WESLEYAN POETRY

A DRIFTLESS SERIES BOOK

This book is the 2010 selection in the Driftless National
category, for a second poetry book by a United States citizen.

EXPOSITION PARK

ROBERTO TEJADA

Wesleyan University Press
Middletown, Connecticut

Published by Wesleyan University Press,

Middletown, CT 06459

www.wesleyan.edu / wespress

2010 © Roberto Tejada

All rights reserved

Printed in U.S.A.   5 4 3 2 1

Library of Congress Cataloging-in-Publication Data

Tejada, Roberto.

  Exposition Park / Roberto Tejada.

    p. cm. — (Wesleyan poetry)

  ISBN 978-0-8195-6932-5 (cloth : alk. paper)

  I. Title.

  PS3570.E435E97 2010

  811'.54—dc22   2009026961

The Driftless Series is funded by the

Beatrice Fox Auerbach Foundation Fund

at the Hartford Foundation for Public Giving.

Wesleyan University Press is a member of the

Green Press Initiative. The paper used in this book

meets their minimum requirement for recycled paper.

NATIONAL
ENDOWMENT
FOR THE ARTS
A great nation
deserves great art.

This project is supported in part by an award
from the National Endowment for the Arts.

Thanks to the publishers of those literary journals, limited-edition chapbooks, and art catalogs, in which some of these works first appeared: *boundary 2*, *Conjunctions*, Galería de Arte Mexicano, *Damn the Caesars*, Galería Nina Menocal, Galería Ramis Barquet, *MiPOesias*, *o•blék*, Phylum Press, *P-Queue*, *The Pulchritudinous Review*, *Rust Talks*, *Sulfur*, Universidad Nacional Autónoma de México (UNAM), and *Viceversa*. The Smithsonian Institution and the Library of Congress kindly provided the photographs that appear in this book.

A very special thanks to Rosa Alcalá, Esther Allen, Joel Bettridge, Susan Briante, Mary Coffey, Kristin Dykstra, Alan Gilbert, Peter Ramos, Suzanna Tamminen, and Susana Tejada, whose insight clarified the conception and architecture of these pages; to Francisco Aragón, for his selfless efforts of community endorsement; and to Gabriel Bernal Granados, whose labor made selected pieces elsewhere intone for Spanish-language publication.

The artist looked for a long time, looked about as though in search of something, and then merely asked, pointing out the vacant space between the two pictures; "And where is the Savior?"

—*Freud*

1

A
R
T

&

I
N
D
U
S
T
R
Y

1.

Is there a difference between this honey, that rain
water, the volcano a sleeping woman?
Is it north to the meadow and can the river be crossed before sundown?
Is there food enough to get us there, some turnips and dried meat?
Are there animals to harm us in the forest?
Can I bring my pistol and slingshot?
Should I put the kettle on before telling the story?
Did we pray before supper and these Thy gifts?
The meaning of the shattered glass and open book?
Why is it winter now over the desert, the cactus field blooming?
Why is the soup cold? My hand still sweating?
Were there stars across in April?
Was it last Tuesday?
Whose voices are these in the Institute?
Work to be done on the table and chairs?
The water you can hear me thinking?
Too late to change my mind?

In the beginning, when the will of the king was rendered and he began to scribble signs across the celestial vault, from the most recondite place surfaced a flame, a dark flame, the Infinite, like a vapor forming in what was still unformed, enclosed within the ring of the sphere, neither white nor black, nor green, nor red, of no color at all. It was only after the flame had assumed its form that it flared the resilient colors and from the innermost recess of the flame emerged a will from which the colors rose to cover everything below.

3.

Keep the eel alive until ready to skin.

Kill it with a sharp blow to the head.

Slip the noose around the eel's head and hang the other end of the cord on a
hook, high on the wall.

Cut the eel skin about 3 inches below the head all around, so as not to
penetrate the gall bladder, which lies close to the head.

Peel the skin back, pulling down hard—if necessary with a pair of pliers—until
the whole skin comes off like a glove.

Clean the fish by slitting the white belly and removing the gut, which lies
close to the thin belly skin.

4.

"Insofar as he is spirit, it is man's misfortune to have the body of an animal and thus to be like a thing, but it is the glory of the human body to be the substratum of a spirit. And the spirit is so closely linked to the body as a thing that the body never ceases to be haunted, is never a thing except virtually, so much so that if death reduces it to the condition of thing, the spirit is more present than ever . . . In a sense the corpse is the most complete affirmation of the spirit."

What the ~~clearing~~ looks like: ~~plush~~ green ~~weave~~ in which the ~~names~~ of ~~things~~ had ceased to matter. A ~~willow~~ there, some ~~birch trees~~, silver as well. A ~~cloud~~ obstructing the ~~sun~~, so that the resulting ~~shadow~~ over the ~~field~~, just ~~beyond~~, is variably ~~stained~~ with ~~nothing~~ less than ~~darkness~~. It's when his ~~slender body~~ happens, enormous ~~hands~~ out to ~~here~~ around me, a ~~rhythm~~ to fill the ~~heretofore~~ unsounded ~~spaces~~ of a ~~daybreak~~ taut with ~~light~~.

6.

Clarity before the bloodshed and the darkness thereafter: my drink my hand my letter, simply this bliss what if the skin by the ear the light on after, the weather? To stave off abandon becoming your body in space and time with my tongue hard shape and all eyes everywhere over and over. About glide and endless motion the smooth hand across the blank page of your evening skin: about the rain, a language of first names when the money ended: about places where the dust had gathered around the broken objects and the cabinets by which they were divided: sustain the wind is blowing hence the clothes hung out to dry a line in the meadow: about this vehicle of the extramural, higher transfiguration of these increasingly fugitive intimacies.

7.

TODAY I SHARPENED MY KNIFE, PICKED 9 PEARS. I WAS WOUNDED BY A SCORPION, PLAYED THE RATTLE, BAKED BREAD, DREAMT OF AN ISLAND IN THE MIDDLE OF A LAKE. AWAKENED, SMOKED A PIPE, SLAUGHTERED A PHEASANT, SPILLED MY ONLY GLASS OF WINE, SLEPT. THIS TIME I DREAMT THE 4 PLANETS LOVED ME IN THEIR ORBIT. THEN I DISAPPEARED INTO THE DARK.

But also the whole Earth in space and time. A record of the rocks, the first living things and life and climate. Age of reptile, mammal and the dawn of the species. The seeds of civilization, early empires, of gods and goddesses and stars, of priest and priestess, queen and king and writing itself. Serf and slave and lord. That garden. This book. The ancients as such. Of princes, parliaments and powers. Of city and State. The orbit around the Sun. Of trade by sea, the Orient, this Terra Nova. All uprising and independence. Factory, machine and earthly paradise. Millenial forebear, animal heart. Wartime entreaty: my voice ••• above the endless racket.

2

GOLDEN AGE

●●●

Lantern that was a lamplight, a clock

Every flickered minute billows into
invisible wind-corpses or flutters,
burning clock, into stirrings flashed
across the very thing you forfeit.
Each glow each sigh and every beam's
a flare of splendors, compliant, if on
the brink of undoing what they grieve by
living what's perished at every passing.
The longer it waxes a winged life—so
death can claim—the greater peril
the clock's to face at its final waning.
Provisional glimmer outburn yourself,
for living longer is with each new death
to embody a view to further deception.

....

Un velón que era candil y reloj

Invisibles cadáveres de viento
son los instantes en que vas volando,
reloj ardiente, cuando vas brillando
contra tu privación tu movimiento.

Cada luz, cada rayo, cada aliento
en ese vuelo de esplendores blando,
va deshaciendo lo que va llorando,
vive lo que murió cada momento.

Cuando durase más su alada vida,
dirá la muerte, más peligros visto
ha este reloj en sus fatales suertes.

Acábate ya, efímera lucida,
que haber vivido más es haber visto
mayores desengaños por más muertes.

[Luis de Sandoval Zapata, 1620?–1671]

•••

If we recognize the variety and groundlessness
of grounds, if we speak from perplexity as
opposed to portrayal, if we are locked into the one
approach dominant in our time when
problems appeared at the periphery, "our distinctions
so that they cut between the bones," can we
promise the standpoint of employing critique
or such assumption as to give voice and image
in light of solace or satisfaction? There is the body
which one and the person for whom.
                                        There's a line
of security glass against handgun, crowbar, baseball bat
is there a bond, any, to what follows

•••

When from my counted days I think of
times still owed to me by tyrant love,
and my temples anticipate a frost
beyond the tribulation of my years
I see love's counterfeit joys are a poison
reason sips from a glass raised
to those for whom hunger dare appear
in the guise of my honeyed daydream.
What potion of forgetting pleases
reason that by neglect of its duty
so toils against itself for satisfaction?
But my affliction seeks solace, measure
of the desire to be remedied and
the desire to overcome it love's remedy

....

Cuando imagino de mis breves días
los muchos que el tirano amor me debe
y en mi cabello anticipar la nieve,
más que en los años las tristezas mías,

veo que son sus falsas alegrías
veneno que en cristal la razón bebe
por quien el apetito se le atreve
vestido de mis dulces fantasías.

¿Qué hierbas del olvido ha dado el gusto
a la razón, que sin hacer su oficio
quiere contra razón satisfacelle?

Mas consolarse quiere mi disgusto,
que es el deseo del remedio indicio,
y el remedio de amor, querer vencelle.

[Lope de Vega, 1562–1635]

•••

The memory of genocide or slavery or sexual
abuse if the former event precludes a claim
if it threatens to destroy me with lesser
arms and munitions over land mines
to blow off the phantom limb of the already
severed self by degrees of experience | Developed
nations later this week out of history endure
in nuclear storming when global theory
and new shapes insurgent welcome
the largest diaspora in the world of who said
can you see the sequoias of California to
Niagara Falls | Trace was the term you erased
in translation | Or was it debt | Was it index

•••

When I stop to consider my calling, remark
the places a wayward temper impelled me
I've found in light of where I wandered lost
the most appalling evils could have befallen;
but when I disregard the journey it's hard to
even fathom I endured so much affliction;
what's more, my days being spent, I feel I've
seen my wariness go with them. I'll come to
my end, for I surrendered artless to someone
with the science to dispel and destroy me if
so inclined, else the know-how to want to;
for if, with this very hand I could slaughter
myself, why—not on my account but because
so suited—would my enemy do otherwise?

....

Cuando me paro a contemplar mi estado
y a ver los pasos por do me han traído,
hallo, según por do anduve, perdido,
que la mayor mal pudiera haber llegado;

mas cuando del camino estó olvidado,
a tanto mal no sé por dó he venido;
sé que me acabo, y más he yo sentido
ver acabar conmigo mi cuidado.

Yo acabaré, que me entregué sin arte
a quien sabrá perderme y acabarme
si quisiere, y aún sabrá querello;

que, pues mi voluntad puede matarme,
la suya, que no es tanto de mi parte,
pudiendo, ¿qué hará sino hacello?

[Garcilaso de la Vega, 1501?–1536]

1.

If someone waits to witness
the aperture of "sullen earth" (whose cloister
is not without entrance)

who inhales the hyacinth (no, cyclamen)
on this rich telluric pillow
so that a ribbon of sleep is secured

around the hair of girls in saffron coats
whose giggle heard from the insular cliff of Aegea
is the thrill of his falling:

first feminine voices of memory
as to unfasten from familiar recitals
inside all closure of thought.

And the scratchy hinges of delight
when he walks into the orchard
and it's the doña's alcove

it's the silver dome
of pear and pomegranate trees in the bare
winter of her governance; all the same

he unveils her body under gown
sips confection so all else but the quince-colored tuft
warm to lips were a bitter cake

as when in the blur of thumbing
her slender breast pressed back she
looked for a moment like a boy.

2.

Her song is artless. Says *"mah th' maed(n) moathe innana."* Says the dock's sway creak tonight: come cradle with me. Thinks of the horses at the shore whose delicate gallop might mingle with the timbre in the pellucid prose of her undoing. Might lessen the divide between all beach & motion of the sea with each Guidonian syllable in the tonic sol-fa of her choosing. Ah! To sip the hot aria of her logick like short breaths from his mouth later buried in the muzzle of her patch. To unravel the equestrian prance of the groin and its equivocal dance-hall back-step side, side, together: whose finale sings Our Lady of the Paragraph scream O please these drunken sailors!

What with the thick immobility of our limbs & the languor
of breath surrendered like these long pulses of afternoon
from the disarrange of the still-crisp bedding we come
to find our selves flung upon. How heavy donning

sweat-speckled surfaces of skin after whose
repose came we tumbling from the vertigo
of a maternal rose unbending's conduit of the mind's
outward blooming & all doors flung open & all curtains

drawn. How declivity blended with spire to resemble
us walking out with her into the abandoned boulevards
of the silver city and the body's final architecture

where threefold ciphers of maternity constructed
of her soul communiqué from Coyolxauqui come
undarken the hard glow this groin light pyramidal

Self-Recognition of the Fish
[after Sandra Ramos]

Unsettled by the semi-darkness of the undersea night, the velodrome and stadium immense against the backspin of the phrases indistinct now as immersed by the reef-cradle undertow, and marveled by these monuments in place of the invertebrate culture unique to saltwater, rewarded as we were with a glimpse into a landscape few of us will ever know, even with these spastic infant limbs, these urges you want to go away, modes of guiding us down a current where—damsels, triggers, lion fish—high quantities of oxygen help to break down the organic molecules into simpler forms for chemical filtration removal, while maintaining an environment conducive to the culturing of large populations of aerobic bacteria in reference to the future of the continent, or so he says, the fundamental problem now being not one of self-recognition, not here or elsewhere, but of union, the duty to combat isolation despite the economic and social difficulties—or so we're convinced, of health and energy for the increasingly complex functions of the state where women will comprise nearly sixty percent of the country's technical force, hold jobs, earn good salaries, and be free and less dependent on men than in a past where news of each house they built was received here as good news, made us proud because we knew the hardships they faced in the construction, truly very difficult for us all, the town we had intended to build there, a project of great social benefit to the entire population for whom pleasure is derived in being spoon-fed and harmless so that one may lead a normal life through the looking glass of containment and aquatic environments—sagittaria, cabomba, vallisneria—now that, to counter silicates producing micro-algae growth and heavy-metals causing invertebrate melt-down, traditional methods will be applied, like those throughout history in cases of highly dangerous diseases, namely the quarantine of those infected, as in the case of cholera, leprosy, and so on, he added, meaning a slow death, a couple of pumps to hum and gurgle in trying to simulate an analogous system of life for those of us inhabitants still left.

Diorama

[after Magali Lara]

1. [Snake]

Can we so name with any certainty as to be proprietors of sight? And does the night watch really matter? Misgivings that insinuate when issued from the animal aspect, intelligence unable to avoid: something we fear because it moves faster, proves more cunning, leads us into situations that belie our brittle nature. As though transcribed into a journal or travel log, subject at breach point, surrounded by flames, in the process of spilling or secreting; occurrence of blaze and blast. In the wound left by these questions—I can't remember what I wanted—such sight as there is rejected to identify with the beast, "I can guide myself by way of touch, through hearing, or with the tongue. But not the eyes."

A borderland state between demise and rebirth: place parallel to childhood where fingers recur those first prohibitions—of mixing and diluting, of wallowing in our own smear—so as to achieve, at last, a change of skin. In the underpinnings and semantic slippage—as totem and taboo, as a figure of movement, as the shorthand for temptation and erotic consequence, as an omen of danger and death, as the simile for writing or as a pattern of abstraction—the snake an endless oscillation of emblem and motif: plasticity itself, in form pliable and by line perverse, in all things deviation, from coiled spiral glyph to ascending fret. *Translucent paper shrunk and crinkled by the wetness of the watercolors, these tendrils and probes.* "One of two folds to surround an opening" and the intellect by way of touch and senses, when the sheltered part of the psyche surges now with a violence demanding a new gauge to measure the categories of a self.

Blur in the borders between determined nature of the symbolic and ephemeral condition of the real: where the outside—unless subsisting inside—is meaningless.

2. [Habitat]

Soy la única que no se mueve.

No hubo quién tras las dos
puertas donde el horizonte
fue el agua
                 derramada
de la lluvia anterior

Columna vegetal la hiedra desde
Uno de los tres jarrones
—como la noche por
el vientre
                 retrato, como
un desierto, el de este sueño
vertido (entre
los árboles) sin
mirar atrás

Supe al fin cómo estaba hecho.

3. [Ice]

decibel thread | mineral spool | entropic blue

mind-line   diamond   willow-wood   gland

tress   headstone   splinter   plunge

rime   grip   spiral   copse

cascade   forefinger   rib-cage   throng

silica of the lungs | half-breed of ground and sea | color of a coma

zodiac   pubis   colony   court

landform   ledger   blemish   orb

monitor   latex   filament   glue

miasma   tissue   cogwheel   speech

short long | long   short short short | long short long short

platform   slashes   tripwire   ink

thumb   cluster   lozenge   loop

anemone   method   number   crust

chalk-circle   category   predicate   sough

Bishopric of Darwin | Narrows of Morse | Inlets of Piaget

wave crest	fracture	semaphore	shell
graphite	tidewater	dioxide	flange
contusion	wax	analgesic	milk
coal	encasing	metal	bone

weight of sapphire | breath below sea level | cargo of division into parts

lifespanoftheharbormaster | daughtersowingtoice | leaguesunderPatagonia

somewhere over this edge | anywhere but here | nowhere near completion

Esemplastic Negativity

[after Melanie Smith]

The things you purchase—place coined from the blunt material-of-the-world, a site unseen of objects inexhaustible, a space of dissembling depth where body-mind and gadget crash in head-on collision—the divide riven between state control and global capital, theater of useless appetites and credit in erratic rates whereby the problem is not one of debt per se, as people are led to suppose—the entire project relying, after all, on repeated deferral for its creativity and progress—blaring integers and agents always saying there will be THINGS YOU CAN'T AFFORD TO LIVE WITHOUT, a sheer empire of orange, hence also of pink and black, in banners hoisted—lozenge, nombril, point, fess—to hail this spectacle of acquisition, as if to say your ability to buy is to be physically desirable, the improved alternative to who you are, an unsettled appetite and pervasive anxiety to obtain the wherewithal whose unqualified role of excess is a more systematic banality to suffer the un-astounding nature of workaday life, of NEW MODELS EXPECTED FOR GROWTH IN ECONOMIC ACTIVITY, as with the intent of looking at art, seen as though you were rendered a potential consumer by the spewing sunshine psychedelic, the firing-squad lined against the body of praxis—an apricot nail-polish sold as Kirchner and O'Keeffe—but on the other hand, towards the idiom of its own manufacture, the precedents of advertising and early development, where two boys confronted with the dubious prospect of a cereal "supposed to be good for you," will pass it on to their younger brother "who hates everything" so that all time and space of the world you inhabit waxes foreign in the hard sell aimed at corporate growth, your sense of significance in the present used for product-positioning via retrieval-cues in the unyielding surface of personal memory and facts amassed over time between or inside out, an expanse and contraction with the music of its referent leading to spontaneous brand awareness by way of image-attribute and compliance, specimens rendered paralytic within the fifteen-second time-spot, as decided by arbiter agents based upon a point system that takes into account the factors of cosmetic aggression or control being defined as any perceived affect upon or alteration—including dents, gouges, holes, lost parts, and so forth—opposed to active subjects, as opposed to being cornered into cultural poverty and emulsified wealth, between what is and what could be, such as whether or not the sponsors invest in the arms trade, support oppressive regimes—THE WORLD IS YOUR UNOCCUPIED GROUND—a series of questions about this rank abundance and utopian lure whereby the majority goes without, or aspires to a modest share of sporting goods, the ubiquitous concatenation of gimcrack trade in purchase and peddle, the seduction by which we are obviated, incrassate polymer thermoplastic squadron where VENDORS WAGE BATTLE AGAINST PUBLIC OFFICIALS OVER RIGHT TO DOWNTOWN STREETS, the operating environment of the screen in relation to packaging and life-style as throw-away goods and teeming containers are to a severed hammerhead in the formaldehyde of television, forms that pacify you in the new wilderness of acetate and vinyl clusters rhyming with the Apollo-nine white noise or the techno-phenol dream of a weight-lifted anatomy in social excellence and juice bars of tangerine and high-octane gulf-war video flamboyance of so much reading matter in reference to proper names in the city of signage, illiteracy and things to buy in the strip of buildings and contaminated light—the cleft self no longer determined at the point of satisfying these elastic urges—the fat life caught between the hard edge of the old and the leisure promise of the new synchronized handling and forceful hum of the right stroke of sexual insolvency—POLYMER NERVE-ENDING IN SHUDDERS OF NEVER ENOUGH TO THE COOL PISTOLS OF BREATH ALONG SPENT FLESH—when financial identity is rendered inviolate at last in the swell of dispossession, no weave or warmth to the colonized colors waved for a sham democracy's parasitic standing.

•••

Leverage for power divided by insight
for intelligence is the crush of a lozenge
—province wherein conflicted
voices say all these awful things
about you have no idea what it means
to be this erratic if church bells
and headlights over Austin winter
traffic stay crisp in tintinnabula of
recorded sound where gentle rain in
pine forest, cityscape in thunder
storm as if ago from book
buying these manuals in repair
of a '69 Peugot 404 sedan—
as head-on in a car-wreck
as by telephone everything
halts these six degrees
                    of

•••

In dreams a joke
slips in his
mouth across
the room and
cats off the building
in fits & starts of
a gravity about
the point—or lack
thereof. To build a less
permanent place
from which to work
while someone
waits for nothing
in particular—a notice
from the bank,
complaints from
a neighbor, approach-
ing guerrillas
slow burn
scoring through

•••

To you my antonym
my gimel from whose
gray arena a man's body
emerges   m   in aftertaste
and edges at the back
of his throat   tongue
sliding between teeth
and gums into daughter-
less corners   His father
plummets: heroic
song thru a wind-
tunnel,   booze + lubricants
choke-chain tighter
his footsteps rising
from my mouth.

•••

Tyranny past participle desire
to please no longer waiting
who if I am all one else's
burned as though to grope in flame
and tongues barely touching
the most insulting paradigms
the other cheek   white beads
of the father when odysseus
and penelope all night all night
under sheepskin covers

•••

Between exuberance and snow
the uncharted world a patrimony
and prayers repeat the ♥ of our
thinking where the eye directs a ☞
to change the world it contemplates
timbre of my own voice: child
of the delirium between us, still-
born: for the exegetes of jesus
to suffer nightless is meaning (so

let the _____ go buried at our feet)

•••

There is someone who knows.

In no beginning
        was there just one language
nor did the surface gleam

with nineteen hours
of music as in our body-heat
through the head & limbs

the thumb and index finger
to form the ovular OH
of our self-fathering fable

war flail ≈ morning star

The original garden erudite,
lush lawn, & round
of trees
behind the limestone square, night

rain out of paper, under
the lights of the narrow
path up the rose hill.

From a dark corner rising now

to write *orange with a knife*
over green of the elusive
wall no one is watching

•••

From otherwise known as stink city or
so by her father, one of other sailors who
said of Texas City, failed mutter, no
nailed to the state of, in scope
and expanse my dirty mouth my
mother loathing nowhere
as it might have been Altaloma
where after

FLOOD

FLAT

FLOOD

goose 49 and I and grandmother Lily
did we salt and strawberry at
her husband every night until supper?
did we sticky taste and Santa Fe
the apostle's creed when she was 5 months
pregnant and the jar
of chigger choke peppers

on account
of which
she gave light
to the idiot son
is what the town folk called him

•••

Converging on scissors
through the table
a door warped by outside noises

inhabitant whose night-spirit animal
meant to be slaughtered
over someone else's fire

not the all-inclusive where-within
that's overthought & wise-sliced
when you know

the shape itself has no
time-lapse between
a music no matter transpires

●●●

To say that the value between given point X and its plane Q shares a likeness to blue conveyed not by "blue" but a nude reposed at his window, the verb to be, or simply the glass of seltzer left untouched at the Savannah Cocktail Lounge, is to arrive at said X taking the mean of all probabilities of blue to which streetlamp, moon, and Thelonious Monk comprise the empty set; and in order finally to calculate the abstract undress one must approach the intellect, so to speak, by way of quotient X whose quantifier A is the emotive tautology when A equals no members of the set "All moons are blue."

•••

subject six seven siblings in remuneration
for services rendered over how many years

[after Millie Chen, Andrew Johnson, and Paul Vanouse]

~ Guidelines for Professional Practices

As a prominent agency with a view both to local and global levels, the Art Institute Service Bureau is resolved to achieve its objective by adherence to the highest professional standards in the implementation of Controlled Lectures and Walking Tours offered to the interpretive community at large. The programs and facilities offered by the Bureau are for the pleasure and edification of the public. This must be recognized by all persons associated with the Bureau but primarily by those responsible for formulating and administering policies and procedures governing the agency. Those individuals affected include the Institute President, Board of Trustees, staff, out-source ministration providers, volunteers, and those who serve on committees or are otherwise associated in an official or professional capacity with the Bureau. These persons have an obligation to preserve and protect this trust.

It is an ethical responsibility of the Bureau to prudently care for, promote, and pass on to posterity all materials employed in its data-outreach programs, lectures and tours. The obligation of the Bureau to its patrons is paramount. The staff shall be in control of all educational components, monitoring the condition and location of these items—the transit path mark, adaptable range finder, identifying flag, and other equipment, as well as all literature provided by the information help desk. Care of the repository includes maintaining information in an orderly and retrievable form, its public availability, and educational programs whereby the public may better appreciate and understand the Service Bureau's mission.

~ Controlled Tour Management Policy

Pleasure and pedagogy are an integral part of the Controlled Lecture and Walking Tours. A primary charge of Bureau professionals is to present the best current information about its activities. Intellectual honesty and objectivity in display and interpretation are the responsibility of every Bureau professional. Staff and volunteers must always maintain the high standards and discipline of their profession while also being mindful that they are employees as well as independent experts. While striving for professional excellence by exceeding expectations, Service Bureau officers must at the same time remember that they are part of a larger institution and must cooperate supportively with their colleagues.

Bodily fitness, visual enjoyment and the claims to social truth are the universal green and pasture-happiness by which the Controlled Lecture and Tours aim to counter a sensation of safety-comfort—an easier life for us all. When the scenery of daily life and the general murmur of the world are discontinuous, when a moving body unlearns its position in public space and the social system that makes transit meaningful, the perceptual nutrients provided by each Tour will track a narrative that tells not only of actual ecological surroundings, built environs, and its human dwellers, but will probe with questions also about the combined impact of these categories en route. How can mapping the history of land-use guide communities to act in view of the cultural sprawl? Can community-work assist to oppose developers, to protect a large part of the landscape as common ground, and to enjoy the land productively in an ecologically sustainable way? Based on practical experience and historical citation, each Tour urges users to go beyond simply preserving open space so as to engage with localities where knowledge can be made available.

It is the duty of Service Bureau professionals therefore to explain in a timely manner the underlying themes explored in the human power-generated cassette-tours. If requested, stewards should illustrate the means by which the expenditure of caloric energy on the Walking Tour will solicit individual effects that include apprehension and misgiving. Insomuch as the content of Tours may pose challenges to Institute patrons, stewards should stress how perceptual or data-driven evidence may or may not translate into a discernment of assumptions. The voice-data recording sound-script on each cassette provides descriptive passages customized for mood-enhancement discontinuous with duration in real time. Each modality—Safe, Natural, Comfortable, Convenient, Controlled, Efficient, Spacious, Diverse, Civilized, Pleasant—may be experienced as either a productive fracture between a patron and his or her environment, or as broadcast sensation-cluster. To counter the latter, art professionals may find it necessary to describe a hypothetical relationship between a walking subject and cultural or natural data received as instrumental message, or as a habit of grammar—that is, in the interval between what an individual believes and how a person is instructed. (Only in exceptional cases will art professionals see themselves obliged to discuss diagnostic skills with an unqualified patron, so disclosing the Institute as already in truck with the motives and gains of said aptitude.)

Stewards are strongly encouraged to emphasize, by way of contrast, that the Institute perspective is life-advancing and species-preserving; that it recognizes the benefits of resisting customary value-sentiments with physical discomfort or limitations that may lead to appetites by which public space may be otherwise imagined. To advance the common good and well-being of its patrons, especially so when expedited by visual logic and artificial soundscapes, is ever contingent upon the degree to which an individual is in command of her emotions—dominant, fecund or subordinate; formative, grounded or inspired; absolute, lifelike or counterfeit. Aware that it is the best knowledge that wants most to hold us to this fabricated world, Institute professionals and patrons are urged to relish in the truth of untruth insomuch as the Institute perspective is to live delighted in the practicable field of sensation and therein the differences between what we see, where the discernible will lead us, and to what degree a single person is able to power the outcome.

[after Thomas Glassford]

D
E
B
R
I
S

I
N

P
I
N
K

A
N
D

B
L
A
C
K

If pink has to be contrasted with black in order to suggest desire, would this black
be black enough had we never thirsted for purity?

—*Bataille*

Objects that hover there above the surface of a subject, kindly as upgrades in urgent care, rescue to make us suspect or safe in the need for shelter, heightened on behalf of a petrifying world, my stomach swelling as it capitulates to onslaught and then I saw it, thought of you my little shame, short of light long in alternating current.

• • •

It's what industry can render of a hard shell with surgical staples clamped across the upturned mouth to keep the cavity shut. I've a lip made bilateral and speech came in time, such that with practice I communicate decidedly. In all truthfulness, in my many-colored murmur, in what nation's accent?

• • •

At the rift of shared beliefs and common artifacts that detach a generation from the world or otherwise shield us from each other by means of learning and geography, is the partition of the nominal, grammar dash or no space; of value, habit, and behavior: *flood-line, blackjack, starburst.*

．．．

What does futility know? What can the divisions remember?

．．．

Insofar as they combine to form the compound nouns, it's the second element that identifies the salient object or person (for instance *man, friend, box, room*), with the first part telling of its aim (as indicated by *police, boy, tool, bed*). Blackout at the looking glass, unite the guest and foreigner, most reflective of feeding time when I swallowed my own likeness.

．．．

We were careful not to say things more than we were to say things.

· · ·

Supposing there are no clear laws about the common combinations—
flowchart, shareholder, money shot, stretch piece—once formed, transmogri-
fied, cut off by a hyphen for a time, then united as one word: *greenhouse,
hardware, rainfall, onlooker.*

· · ·

Extent of a lifespan: degrees of undefined space.

· · ·

If each gap imparts an opportunity for error, the closed form melding
together into *secondhand, childlike, crosstown*; or sidelong into *master-at-
arms, over-the-counter, mass-produced, self-sovereign*, when not the open form
inclusive of *real estate, middle class, half moon, attorney general.*

• • •

Congenital lesion: unbridled grounds; the 500 years the 300 families.

• • •

When masculine and feminine modify the environs, fifth power compelled to disintegrate in cataclysm, moving parts challenged by an ever-present forecast, parcels of land between the mountains, combatants falling like petals. One day, describe it in the present for your name to outlive you, the stars discharging or whatever.

• • •

Encompassing crest, crumbling relic: estranged from the places I was meant to address.

• • •

Membrane, make an effort to efface a feeling, now and then, of remorse for actions whose guilt I assumed from time to time as liability, a sort of quest or confusing narrative hanging at mid-breath, somehow never finding a finality or conclusion, yet seemingly specific in detail and urgent in command.

. . .

Precarious conviction: common hemorrhage: suspended shape.

. . .

If you pass for heterosexual, separate pink from the 50,000 tongues and a flimsy swath of fabric, hard part for lips gorged on a load as though starving to death in such deep action slit wide open for close up shots that resound around an outline for a number of us, fingers wet, faces tight with surge and stain.

. . .

What means this infraction: you fuck now: me nothing-to-declare.

. . .

In efforts to poison water and air, escape regulation and silence critics, was employed the technology to consolidate a blue-collar constituency of truckers and housewives, not to speak of deviants who snorted, swallowed or injected, to the degradation of those areas of the brain associated with feelings of euphoria.

. . .

Please ascend out of this narcosis, sweetheart, into the form and value of interrogation skills, conduct deemed heinous and unlawful only when wrought by individuals; state flow blocked in ordinance of horizontal increase by means of arteries, stretched the length of my neck, vessels that harness sufficient blood to the head.

. . .

Daylabor ante, checkpoint tease: identification at all times.

. . .

Lost in downward spiral, impaled by a series of rods clamped between next of kin and state to make palpable a time in history when what the world measured of an uncommon life was secretly familiar, exacting of a stamina by which, wired and gaunt, those formerly withdrawn gain self possession such that productivity improved at the work place.

. . .

What does self-possession contain? Radiant barricade: half-strangled moan.

. . .

Neither slain nor eaten in final distend or radical relaxing, irrefutable tools for building the house of behavior in the family relation, fiscal exchange and legal sanctions that fashion the subjects of money and bylaws, or I am a believer when the angel of elation sayeth unto me: *slash, thrive, overcome, withhold.*

· · ·

Because no scientific consensus can be reached, because patients continue to suffer, enhanced methods notwithstanding, because there are only so many stretchers and the institution understaffed, what cannot yield is a form of authority, dear porcelain sheen when sutures sustain the tissue.

· · ·

Labors erased in the telling; lives unruffled by war.

· · ·

Anodized aluminum security access and attaché, sleek detector in a mine-field deterrent of biological assault, bodies fit for fear, repression and denial, protective device and life support system threatened by chemical effect, sexual infection, totemic club, and nightstick concealed or ascending to the glandular sun.

· · ·

Do not fail to corroborate the following: *a)* skin color *b)* land use *c)* passport.

· · ·

Lactic, ineffaceable, and subterranean, diffuse on such a massive scale as criminal behavior is to a world fitful with suicide bombs on Tuesday, chrome metals rekindled in the populace, speech accountable to the district like money pledged as security for foodstuff, thick with carbonates and alkaloids, electrolytes and protein.

· · ·

Insofar as the margins between mirror and method double over, firm digi-tal insertion performed with the purpose of clearing the fluid sac to elimi-nate built-up secretion, empty the organ of dead cells to relieve symptoms when the levels come apart, albeit obedient to the unforeseen emergency of uncertain settlement.

· · ·

The developers, who insinuate what all the others unbuild, confer as
though form were an obstacle.

· · ·

Girdle, surrender your tassels and aperture, barriers dissolved in the vul-nerability of night, invariable domain of attitude and action, influence of the dominant style that comes to the forefront when not otherwise subor-dinate and therefore bound to collapse.

· · ·

This is to say the pleasure it once provided approximate to her body, maternal volume existing nowhere sooner than it was lost to me in a world uncovered not by means of it encroaching but in the compulsion to recur what I forgot I always wanted.

· · ·

Repeat after me: inhale, awaken, and restrain—Broadcast that forbids to lay claim on the inflicting source, strap tethered with the intention to incite the flailing self now inferior, now supreme, surrendering endurance of a body's appetite in pink and black entangled, spent, encased, uncontainable.

Art & Industry: A chief participant in the world fairs of the late nineteenth and early twentieth centuries, Mexico figured prominently in the Exposition of the Three Americas (New Orleans, 1885); the World Exposition (Paris, 1889); the World Columbian Exposition (Chicago, 1892–1893); the Pan-American Exposition (Buffalo, New York, 1901), and the Louisiana Purchase Exposition (St. Louis, Missouri, 1904). Tied to commercial incentives, modernization, and a style of utopian globalism, exhibits and glass cases pictured nation and culture as a theater of folkways. In 1885, writing on the Mexican exhibits at the New Orleans Exposition of the Three Americas for *Harper's Weekly*, Lafcadio Hearn wrote: "These wonderful figurines in wax, representing the various types, callings, costumes, and manners of the Mexican people [. . .] may be studied almost exhaustively through the clear glass of the cabinets." History, language, ethnicity, and landscape appeared in scenes recounting the varieties of civilization, but also as support for a single storyline deployed in existing theories of human development. In equivocal resemblance and arrant contrast to those occasions of display, the tableaux of "Art & Industry" derive from sources, direct and indirect, that include: Moses de Leon, *The Book of Splendor* [2], Irma S. Rombauer and Marion Rombauer Becker, *The Joy of Cooking* [3], Georges Bataille, *Theory of Religion* [4], Roberto Turnbull, *Monotipos* (1991), Galería de Arte Contemporáneo, Mexico City [7], and H. G. Wells, The *Outline of History: Being a Plain History of Life and Mankind* [8].

Golden Age: This sequence travels backward in time by way of a reversed transatlantic passage from New Spain to its colonial center, inasmuch as Luis de Sandoval Zapata was a native of seventeenth-century Mexico; at successive intervals are two thirteen-line sonnets from the chronological present. In *La expresión americana*, José Lezama Lima held human history to be a stage whereon actors perform as "metaphoric subjects" conferred with the task of enacting change in terms of a regenerate view. Elsewhere he submitted as well that "The image is the secret cause of history." The timing of translation, like any measurement of when and where to act, matters deeply to the ethics and energies of a language and its culture. If translation is relevant to both avant-garde and vernacular traditions, one can turn to material counterparts in the image world at large. Subjected to hardship and labor, native artisans in seventeenth-century Oaxaca so specified their indigenous bodies as to flourish in the form of cherubic faces that beautify the ceiling of Santo Domingo Church. In the 1970s, Brazilian artist Cildo Meireles surreptitiously silk-screened messages onto Coca-Cola bottles—"Yankee Go Home"—before re-releasing each container back to its designated course. These being wartime translations and a hybrid text, poetic license doubles therefore as a kind of disobedience.

Self-Recognition of the Fish: In her 1997 installation *Autorreconocimiento del pez* at the Galería Nina Menocal in Mexico City, Cuban artist Sandra Ramos created a three-dimensional self-portrait using camera-generated body-shots of her head, hands, and feet. These appeared superimposed on the glass backing of five aquariums each containing a live goldfish, interconnected with plastic tubing and mirrored panels to complete a bodily outline on the gallery wall. In statements, Ramos relates how these materials were meant to address the effects of mass exile as experienced from within Cuba's socialist project, and of the decision, both political and cultural, to remain in view of that exodus.

Diorama: The three-sided poem corresponds to different bodies of work by Mexican artist Magali Lara: *Serpiente*, Museo de Arte Carrillo Gil (1998); *El árbol del cuerpo*, Galería de Arte Mexicano (1994); *Glaciares*, a single-channel video, 7:47" (2009). In a range of media—painting, drawing, the artist book, and moving image—Magali Lara produces violent distortions that, in a manner of pictorial *écriture féminine*, can graft plant life to animal attribute, vegetable tissue to flesh, barrenness to proliferation, and exuberance to austerity. A composite question compels this work: What markings make legible an emotion, or so ground it as to be sufficient to its life form?

Esemplastic Negativity: In 1994–1996, British artist Melanie Smith turned to sites of exchange on the streets of downtown Mexico City. In a collecting practice restricted to the color orange, the artist scoured through a profusion of mass-produced synthetic objects sold in the casual marketplace composed of street vendors and local retailers. The artist bought these items en masse and assembled the resulting accruals into an ultra-mix of wall sculptures and photographs, into such environments as insinuated by the title *Orange Lush*. Smith upended any compulsory cause-and-effect link between modes of production and the activities of consumption, between sensual appeal and purchasing potential, or between social contract and the dislocated world economy.

Walking Tour: An earlier version of this piece appeared in vehicle-specific relation to *PED.Buffalo* (April–July 2001), a collaborative undertaking conceived by Millie Chen, Andrew Johnson, and Paul Vanouse. As per the artists' statement, *"PED.Buf-*

falo took place at the University of Buffalo Art Gallery and explored pedagogical issues of guidance and control. It posed and answered questions concerning the relationship between the suburban university and the decaying rust-belt city of Buffalo as participants traversed bike paths running throughout the 1200-acre campus, each tour with a different theme based on familiar adjectives used in marketing suburban property. The lectures varied in nature from the professorial to the sensorial, from the informational to the irrational, and periodically disseminated details related to the passing terrain—former wetlands that were paved over to build the campus."

Debris in Pink and Black: For InSite 2005, a transnational public arts project between the cities of San Diego and Tijuana, artist Thomas Glassford worked with landscape architect José Parral to create *La esquina/Jardines de Playas de Tijuana*. This community garden, located in Tijuana's northwest corner, features an elevated platform that provides a view of the U.S. Borderfields State Park, "its massive acreage and estuary beyond," as indicated by Glassford, "in deep contrast to the overpopulated foothills and parched landscape of Tijuana." Also unavoidable was the display of "the Gulf War tarmac fence [that] plunges into the waves of the Pacific [in] what has become one of the most iconic man-made divisions and borders in the world today." The location is a departure point to further explore Glassford's artworks with the aid of compound nouns that speak to the indeterminacies of adjacent materials and ambivalence prompted by the sexualized gaze.

Roberto Tejada is a visual arts critic, photography historian, and curator. He is currently associate professor of art history at the University of Texas, Austin. He is the author of a book of poetry, *Mirrors for Gold* (Kruspkaya, 2006), and two chapbooks, *Amulet Anatomy* (Phylum, 2001) and *Gift + Verdict* (Leroy Press, 1999). His book, *National Camera: Photography and Mexico's Image Environment*, studies art historical episodes in relation to visual documents and local identities in Mexican and U.S. culture (University of Minnesota Press, 2009); he continues to co-edit the journal *Mandorla: New Writing from the Americas*.

The Driftless Series is a publication award program established in 2010 and consists of five categories:

DRIFTLESS NATIONAL, for a second poetry book by a United States citizen

DRIFTLESS NEW ENGLAND, for a poetry book by a New England author

DRIFTLESS ENGLISH, for English language poetry from an author outside the
    United States

DRIFTLESS TRANSLATION, for a translation of poetry into English

DRIFTLESS CONNECTICUT, for an outstanding book in any field by a Connecticut
    author

The Driftless Series is funded by the Beatrice Fox Auerbach Foundation Fund at the Hartford Foundation for Public Giving. For more information and a complete list of books in The Driftless Series, please visit us online at http://www.wesleyan.edu/wespress/driftless.